Kisses from Kale

Disclaimer

The poems in this book are true stories – things Kale
actually did. Very few are exaggerated at all – she really is
as smart and hilarious as she sounds in these poems. She
truly does have such a big personality, as portrayed in this
book. That is why I had to write this book – it was too good
not to. I know that many other dog lovers will relate to these
poems, and for those who don't, well, you can live vicarious-
ly through Kale's stories.

Copyright Information

Kisses from Kale: a collection of poems and memoirs

Copyright © 2023 by Victoria Gehman

Cover and Illustrations by: Madeline Gehman
Interior Formatting by: KJ Robinson, kjrobinsonpoetry.com
Author photo on back cover by: Alana Blythe Visuals

ISBN: 979-8-218-30690-8

Dedicated to:

Kale Mocha, Gracie, Ellie Mae, Lexie, Sophie, Maddy, Misty, Daisy, Katie, Becky, Maya, Ellie, Lily, Bert, Hank, Adler, Thor, Bambam, Remy, Porter, Lilly, Dewey, Caesar, and all the dogs I've ever loved and will love in the future

Also Dedicated to:

April, who was the best foster mom for Kale and so many others until they found their forever homes. Thank you for enjoying the (nearly) daily doses of Kale photos I send you. I love that we share such a deep love for doggos, and I am so grateful for you. Thanks for being one of the first to enjoy these poems.

A huge shoutout to Shelby Leigh and the Poetry Club for providing a community of fellow authors to support one another. So many of you have encouraged me in my work, and it is in the poetry club that I met KJ Robinson, without whose expertise, this book would not be what it is today.

A special thank you to my advanced readers:
Eric, Summer, Valerie, KJ, Victoria, Laurel, Liz, April,
Carissa

Early Reviews:

"Kisses from Kale is a sweet, witty, and heartwarming collection of poems that any dog owner can relate to. The shifts in perspective gives the reader a glimpse into Kale's thinking, motives, passions, and love for her family. This book shows the positive impact that our pets can have in our lives and how much their unconditional love can be forever etched onto our hearts." – Carissa

"These are so precious. I could literally see and feel the puppy love from the first poem in the book. The poems capture dog silliness and affection so well." -Liz

"I laughed and I cried..." -April

"I thoroughly enjoyed every poem...Any dog parent will enjoy reading this...Would be a great gift for the holidays." -Eric

2.16.22

the day my life forever
changed for the better
because that's the day i first wrapped you in my arms
letting you know you were safe from any harms
you got off that truck
and into my arms you jumped
you hugged and kissed me right away,
longing to believe you're here to stay
you knew i was your mom just from the facetime calls
and on my shoulders you put your paws.
[our first hug]

create a new record

i'm going to need
you to create a new record
for oldest dog to ever live
because without you –
i couldn't live
[why don't dogs have the lifespan of humans]

you are safe now, mommy

moths are scary
must protect mommy at all costs:
will climb walls, rearrange living room furniture,
whatever it takes to protect you, mommy.
see, i growl at them
and hunt them down
until they are dead.
you are safe now, mommy.

you gave me purpose

you gave me purpose –
someone to come home to;
your excitement to see me each day
was what kept me going.
on days i wanted to die,
i had to stay
because you needed me;
you gave me purpose.

why i work

to work i must go -
to provide for the family
so you have food to eat,
a house in which to sleep,
fun things to do
and bones to chew,
the best life i can give you.

the lamp

you glared at me
with a stamp of disapproval
before you turned off my lamp

you talked to me
before you inched that paw
towards the cord

you flipped the switch
and i know you knew
what you were doing

you curled up in bed
and ignored what i said
about how mommy is in charge of the lamp

and if we still had any doubts about your level of
smartness,
well, you did it three nights in a row,
which goes to show: you knew what you were doing

and you wanted that lamp off
so mommy had to go to bed
at the same time as you,

all curled up lying next to me,
i left that lamp be,
and i just snuggled up to you.

they got it all wrong

they say i rescued you
but we both know you rescued me, too.
your love is so pure,
and of your loyalty, i am sure.
you gave me purpose, a reason to come home.
i am no longer ever alone.
i think they got it all wrong –
you were the rescuer all along.

first lab love

my love for labs –
it goes way back.
Lexie was my first partner in crime.
by my side all the time,
we were inseparable.
after her, it was only inevitable
that i would need dogs for the rest of my life
no matter the strife
at times they do cause –
the mischief and the muddy paws –
their love trumps any inconvenience
and their existence
is the greatest gift we could ever receive;
that's why when they're gone, we endlessly grieve.

our engagement story through the eyes of Kale

when mommy got engaged of course you were there
he took awhile to get through his speech.
you yawned three times, as if to say
"come on, this is not how we rehearsed it;
just ask the question already."

when he finally got down on one knee and opened that
little ring box
you jumped up
like you wanted him to put the ring on your snout
as if to say "me and my mommy – we are a package."
he knows, Kale, he knows.
then you stood there confused, wondering why we are
crying while doing our favorite adventure,
you looked at us like "come on, let's go."
mommy hugged you tightly and exclaimed her
excitement.
you just wanted to chew the stone off the ring.

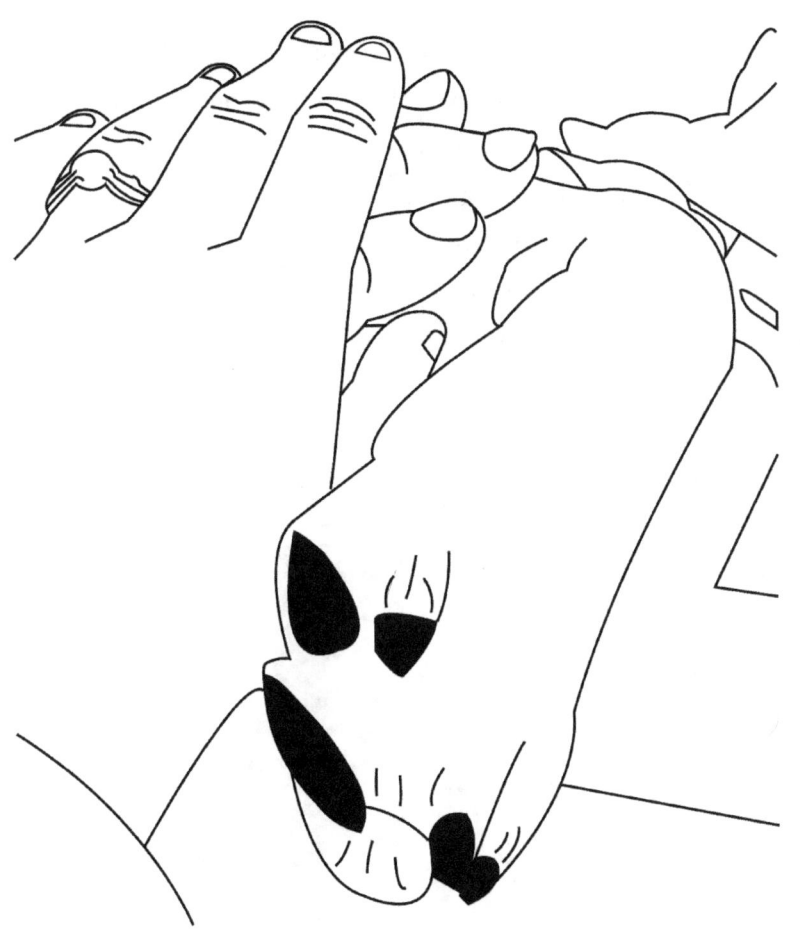

love at first sight

"do you believe in love at first sight?" they asked.
if you're talking about dogs, then yes. yes, i do.
because i knew Kale was the one the moment i saw her
picture on the adoption site
i loved her instantly and effortlessly
so yes, i believe in love at first sight –
but only if that love has paws.

break ups

we could never break up – even if we wanted to.

the girls are so attached,

they would be devastated,

and surely, Kale would take matters into her own paws

and break down your door

and drag you back to me.

to the ones who've gone before

when you get there,
will you find all the ones i've loved?
tell them how much i miss them?
especially Lexie. find her first.
tell her i still have that hippo i used to snuggle with her
when we were both babes.
tell her i miss reading books to her, but i now read to
my own pup.
tell her she'll always be the one that made me such a
dog lover.
tell her your photo and hers now sit side by side,
and i think you'd make great friends.
take care of each other up there,
until i get there.

never pee alone

first one, then two, then three
doggie snouts
push open the door.
mom, you watch us pee and poo,
and we must watch you, too.
[you'll never pee alone again]

4am

it's 4am
and i'm awoken
by a little poke from your cold wet nose
and one single whine
i ask you what is wrong
nothing was wrong –
you just wanted to snuggle with your mommy.
that's so sweet –
but it's 4am
could we maybe wait 'til a more reasonable hour?
i say as i pull you close and give you a belly rub.

she chose me

it was love at first sight
for Ellie Mae
on that day
all felt right.

after seven long years
with only a father
she said, "hear, hear,
dad, i need a mother."

she followed me all around
when i would leave the dog park,
oh you should have heard her sounds
"take me home," she would bark.

so, one day i did.
and that was the beginning of it all —
she became my kid
and in love her dad and i did fall.

and you better believe
she saved up all her drama
for now she had a mama.
and she takes great pride in the fact
that she chose me to join the pack.

begging

mommy, that steak
the one right there on your plate –
it looks really scrumptious,
like it's ready for german shepherd consumption
and for labrador testing.
our mouths are watering,
hoping you'll give in, we're sitting real still
if you don't share soon, we'll go in for the kill:
snatch that steak
right off the plate;
faster than you can say no,
down our throats it will go.
[three cute begging faces staring up at mom's food]

taste tester

when mommy brings pupcups home from work,
you rate them on a scale of 0 wags to 10 wags.
you do the sniff test –
fresh pupcups get tail wags before you dig in,
if they're not fresh enough for your liking, you look at
me with sad eyes and refuse to eat it, spitting it out so
it rolls across the room.
and for the freshest ones of all, you reserve extra tail
wags and a run around the house before you take your
treat away to enjoy it in privacy.
[someone hire this girl right now as a pupcup taste tester]

saturday morning snuggles

there is one day each week
where mom's alarm doesn't go off
and we get longer to sleep

i love those days because it means we get extra cuddles
i lay on mommy's chest and she wraps me in her arms
she likes to call this "saturday morning snuggles."

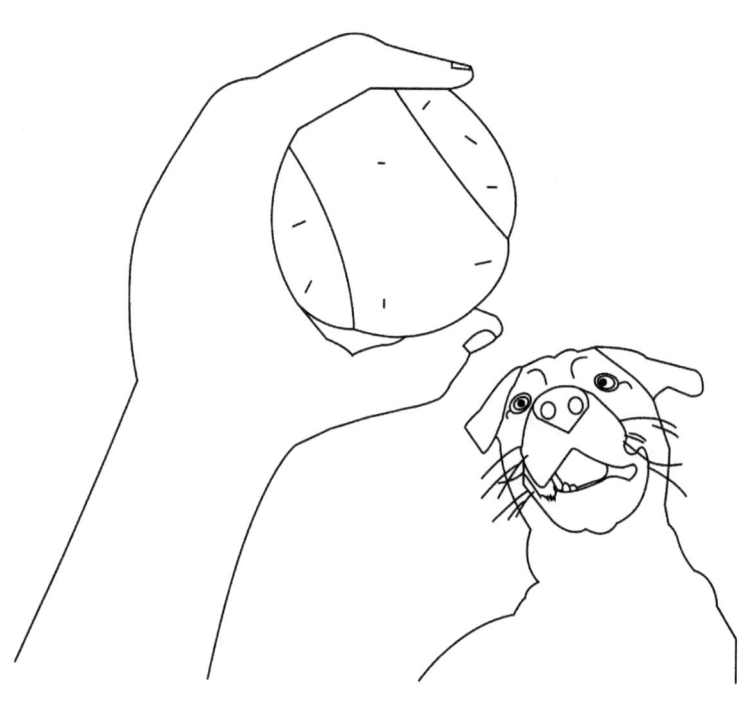

glow in the dark ball

Kale, the reason i bought you a glow in the dark ball
was not so that you could wake me at 2am
demanding that i throw it down the hall.

kibbles and bits vs blue buffalo wilderness

for thirteen years, i've been fed the doggy equivalent of
mcdonalds –
oh, the insult!
when i could have been eating fancy food.
oh, the pandemonium that ensued.
my mommy introduced me to the best
and i made my dad buy it for me for what's left
of my life
i will do anything for even one bite –
climb couches, bite tables,
anything to get as much fancy food as i am able.

frying pan

i have only a couple bad habits –
like yanking mom's arm nearly out of the socket,
hunting for rabbits.
like stealing dirty dishes out of the sink
quicker than you can even blink.
i'm so considerate though –
i bring the frying pan down low –
onto the floor where my sisters can reach
so we all get a few bites to eat.

dogsitter

the night before my first sitter came
i spent all evening sharpening my teeth
i chewed ten different bones
just to be sure they were sharp as could be.

the morning my first sitter came,
my mommy asked me if i was going to be a good girl
i sighed a deep sigh,
"i guess if i have to, mom."

when my first sitter arrived,
i shocked everyone by being such a very good girl,
but, i did try to push her off the bed that night.
she needed to know it was my bed, and a privilege to
share it with me.

fly you a sitter (a haiku)

you're such a handful
i have to fly a sitter
from alabama

<u>sense of smell</u>

if at any point in the last fifteen years,
there was a squirrel that climbed that tree,
i will sniff it out
and tell you all about
the squirrel – where it hid its acorns
which branches it climbed, and whether i could have
caught it.

sisters

we're not from the same litters,
but they are my sisters.
whether hiking, napping, or truck rides
we're always side by side.
like human sisters, we sometimes fight
but we always make things right.
we scheme together to get more foods –
one distracts, while the other snatches the goods.
we put our heads together, looking up at dad and mom
because three dogs begging is more effective than one.
we share the same toys; we trade our bones.
if my sisters are here, i am always at home.

head of security

i am head of security;
you placed something new
in german shepherd territory;
must go check it out
sniff, sniff,
okay that's fine, i guess.
but that deer head on the wall –
that is not okay.
that poses a threat,
maybe partially – or even mostly –
because that head –
it kinda resembles mine, just a bit
and why would we be hanging german shepherds heads
on the walls in german shepherd territory?
will bark at it every night around 12:00 am
to ensure they don't suddenly come to life
and pose a threat to my household.
because i am head security.

self-esteem

i have high self-esteem
because every day, my mom –
she tells me that i am the most beautiful girl
in the whole entire world.

do you...

when i say the words "do you..."
you fling your head around,
as if you heard a startling sound.
you know the words to follow will be:
"want to go on a walk?"
"want to go on a hike?"
"want to go to the mountains?"
"want to go to the dog park?"
"want to visit friends?"
"want to chew a bone?"
"want to have snuggle time with mommy?"
and your answer to each one will be a resounding yes,
as you jump up in the air, your excitement you express.

kisses

i love it when i kiss you goodnight and your fur tastes
like trees and woods and smells of campfire and fresh
mountain air.
[you are my mountain pup]

barky bark

no need to bark
the neighbors can also go on a walk,
just like we do,
they are allowed to go outside, too.

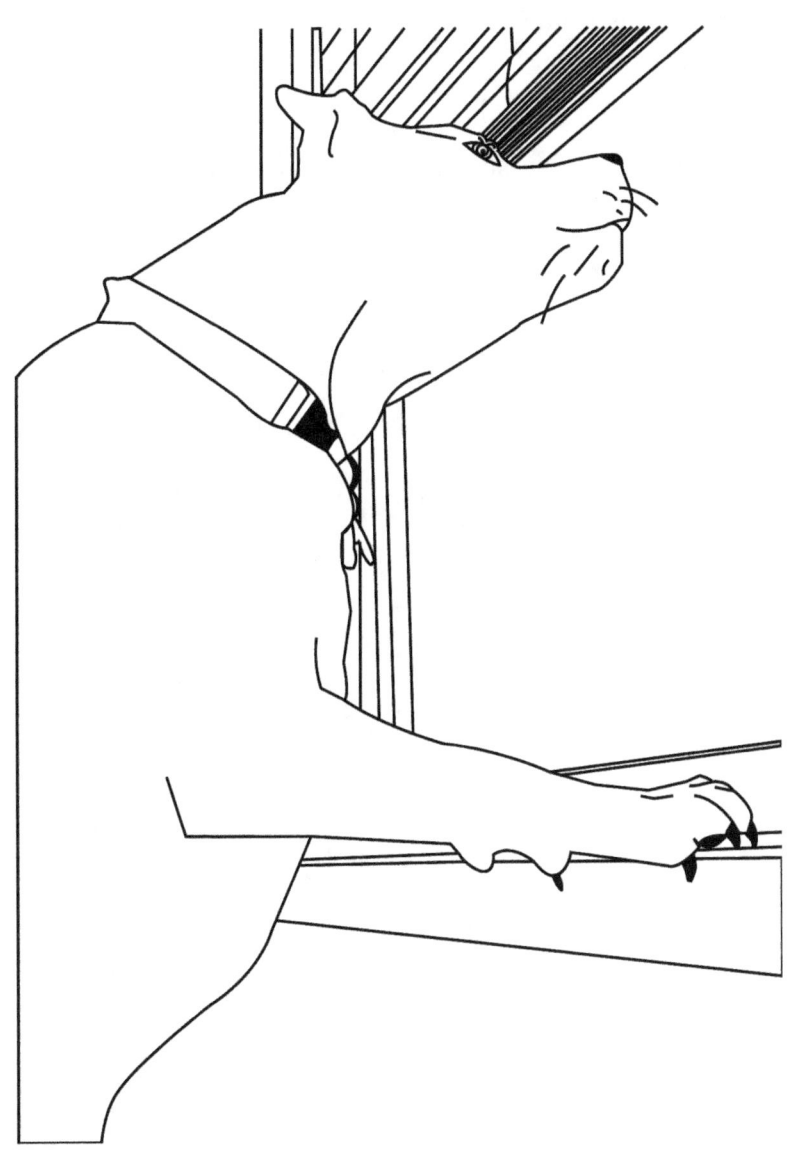

now we both have anxiety

i needed you for emotional support
but now i'm just paying for meds for the both of us.

the vet

my dear sweet pup,
if you hate the vet,
i recommend that next time you drop the tennis ball
instead of swallowing it whole.
i know you didn't want me to take it,
but surely that would have been a better option than
getting so sick.
because now x-rays show it's in your tummy
and at 3am we're stuck in this exam room, and you say
it's no longer so yummy
you think this sucks
and I agree - it'll cost at least a couple thousand bucks.
and probably a few years off my life
for this was a lot of worry and strife.

the atrocity: ran out of bones

i'm sorry girls, i don't know how i allowed this to
happen,
but we basically have no bones left in this kitchen
mommy will rectify this in the near future, i promise.
however, Ellie Mae, you could have stopped at one
"but mom, that would have been no fun."

when i got a dog i didn't know that i was also getting...

-a german shepherd security system

-a vacuum cleaner

-a window washer

-a dish washer

-a newborn

-a toddler

-a teenager

-an interior designer (aka wrecks the house)

-and most of all, a best friend

names i call my dog

Kale
Kale Mocha
Kale Mocha Bear
Mochi Bear
Scooby Doo
Kale Mocha Scooby
Sweetie
Kale Kale
Kale baby
Beautiful girl
[because are you really even a dog mom if you don't
have at least ten different names you call your pup]

ghost

[i accidentally taught Kale that fixing the bed
means it's time to play ghost].
when my fiancé was fixing his bed,
Kale climbed up and grabbed the sheets,
hiding underneath.
he said "what's her problem?"
i said "oh, you didn't ask her if she wanted to be a
ghost.
sorry, but you're going to have to do that every time
you fix the bed for the rest of her life."

what's it like living the dream

tell me: what's it like?
what's it like never having to grow up and get a job,
your food appearing like clockwork every day,
spending your days adventuring, eating, sleeping, and
playing,
always being a dog child,
tell me: what's that like?

kisses from Kale

because i've never met a girl who gives as many kisses
as you do.
to both animals and humans.
nearly everyone you meet is deserving of your love –
what if we all lived a little more like that?
even if they don't want your love,
you force it upon them.
it's like you want everyone to know – both man and
beast – that they are beloved.
and i love that about you.

progress

you used to be terrified of the car or any moving
vehicle;
now, you run errands with me everywhere
and you've become the mountain neighborhood ATV
pup.
you beg for rides each morning
and my heart melts a little
to see how far you've come.
so, of course, i oblige
and take you for a ride.

tennis court

there's a tennis court behind our house
sometimes they hit the balls over the fence
and when they land in our yard,
to guess what happens next is not hard
i claim them immediately –
now those tennis balls belong to me.
look mommy, it's brand new and bright,
and if it's in my yard, to keep it is my right.

fur-niture

she thinks she owns every piece of furniture in this
home
and at this point, she probably does.
because when she barks, demanding my chair, i move,
for the queen must have her rightful throne.

too young to date

Kale, you're only one year old. that's too young, i said.
but when i saw the depths of their love,
there was nothing i could do
but exclaim "aww!" and agree:
yes, Bert can be your boyfriend.
he always smells so good.
he's oh so handsome.
and he even shares his favorite sticks with you.
he is the goodest boy.
and if i had to choose a boyfriend for you,
i couldn't have done a better job –
i will gladly make Bert my son-in-law.
now, when are you getting a ring on your snout?

[what dogs do on dates]

-go on evening walks together

-hold paws

-dog park dates

-crash each other's private pool parties

-hug, kiss, and wrestle

-find the biggest stick, break it in half, and give one half to their partner

<u>Sophie</u>

when she'd hear the spoon stirring against my coffee
cup,
she would come running, my sweet pup
for she knew that it was time
to go sit on the deck in the sunshine.

i swear she is part human

yes, i talk to her like she's a human.
because in between all the chewin' and the zoomin'
she's so smart
and has the biggest heart.
i tell her about my day,
i explain what it means to sit and to stay,
i ask her what she wants to do.
give her options of which bone to chew.
she nods her head yes or shakes it no.
she waits until i say "go."
she imitates the faces
mommy makes.
she has her own big personality –
i'd say she takes after me, if you spend enough time
with us, you'll see –
both stubborn and sweet,
will do most anything for a treat.
except the vet –
that makes her fret.
no peanut butter will she take out of their hand.
she knows all the tricks, and her ground she will stand.
i once told her we couldn't go on a walk because it was

stormin.'

she ran to the window to check if i was lyin.'

she understands and hangs on every word i utter.

if she doesn't like it, she will whine and mutter.

she talks back like a child,

and sometimes she can be a little wild.

she's recently learned how to spell,

and only time will tell

just how much

this pup

is capable of accomplishing

after she finishes the demolishing

of my furniture.

i may be broke financially, but because of her love i am
richer.

Maddy

my first chocolate lab love:

i dogsat her so often i joked i should have partial

custody,

spent many a holiday with her.

she comforted me through tears, and we enjoyed

adventures together.

she loved car rides the most but would whine at any

red light that lasted too long –

just wanted to keep moving.

she was hilarious, too –

if i was gone at work too long, she'd let me know.

but not the way you'd think –

she would steal something left on the counter

(a loaf of bread or a bag of goldfish).

but she – surprisingly – wouldn't eat it.

she would simply carry it up the stairs and leave it

there.

for me to find outside the bedroom door.

she left us way too soon and never got to meet my

Kale,

but a place in my heart she'll always hold.

my Maddy girl.

release

slipping off her harness each night,
imagining it is the same kind of release
we women feel when we unhook our bras
at the end of a long day.

freedom

i slipped my leash today.

through the woods, i ran, free.

i had such a great time, hunting animals, exploring new trails, sniffing all the scents.

i heard my mommy screaming, but i didn't know what was wrong.

i knew where i was all along.

but when i came back, she's nearly in tears,

all sorts of fears

have been running through her head,

fears of losing me.

she says to never do that again,

but i was having the time of my life,

running wild and free.

and i will definitely do it again.

Victoria Gehman

all is right in my world

her back pressed against mine,
now i be feelin' fine
when she sleeps like this all night,
everything in my world is all right.

worse than parents

"that's too close, you need more space between you.
i think i'll just squeeze myself right in here, too"
as she shoves her snout and then her entire body
between us, stares us right in the face.
making sure we know our place.
and curfew is 9:00, on the dot.
i will kick you out on the spot,
see you to the door.
drag you across the floor.
i just wants to see you "out that door...bye, bye, bye"
"mommy, play the NSYNC song i like because he needs
to go now and not a minute later, i cry."
bye bye bye.
don't stop to kiss my mom
or i will lose my calm.
no goodnight kisses for you,
just a little nibble on your chin, from me to you.
[she is worse than parents]

9:00 nips

those little nibbles you give him on his chin,
when you're ready for him to head home,
we call those 9:00 nips.
i wanted to see if you knew what that meant
so i told you to go give him a 9:00 nip,
and straight for his chin you went and gave him a little
nibble.
you know exactly what it means and you know exactly
what you're doing at 9:00pm every evening.
what are you going to do, my dear, when i marry him
and you can no longer kick him out
every night at 9:00 on the dot?
"well mom, then i will simply steal his side of the bed,
every night
and nip if he tries to fight."

Victoria Gehman

kind pup

at the dog park, she's the referee,
if anyone gets out of line, she'll see.
she runs up and down the field,
acting as a shield.
she's kind
to the pups who can't seem to quite find
their place -
she'll give them space,
or she'll invite them to play
"come with me," she'll say
she'll even let them catch the ball,
though she could easily catch them all.

chompy chomp

the way you clamp down
just out of excitement,
you'd have made such a good police dog,
but our friends are not intruders,
or murderers,
so we don't chompy chomp on them.
we only chompy chomp on our bones, our food, or on an
intruder.
and for the thousandth time, mommy's fiancé is not an
intruder.

<u>worth it</u>

when i brought you home
it was about your fifth one
you had so much trauma
and you caused a lot of drama.
countless sleepless nights,
getting you to calm down and sleep was constant fights
i was so exhausted, crying in the car
any progress seemed so far
out of reach.
no matter how much i would beseech
you to please, please be calm
i could not seem to find anything to serve as a healing
balm.
you chewed and destroyed half my home
even though i provided you with plenty a new bone
you were so anxious and terrified by so much:
the car, the groomer, separation, an unfamiliar touch
and especially, the vet – you would not even enter –
and if i tried to force you into the veterinary center
you would growl and snap as though i were going to
hurt you.

i did not understand how to best help you.
but somewhere along the way,
you realized you were here to stay.
we found new rhythms and routines
so much work was done behind the scenes.
it took much love and patience,
but you were worth all the efforts
and now, as i recall the hard days we've overcome
i simply think of how worth it they have become
you taught me how much love
i am capable of.

adventure buddy

who else in your life is always available and always
down for an adventure but a dog?
Kale never says she's too busy for a hike
or that she would no longer like
to spend time with her mom.
she's my forever adventure buddy.

dog park

sitting at the dog park
waiting for friends
i hear a bark
but no dog descends
mommy, i am an extrovert
i need some socializing
mommy sends a text to my friends' moms, including my
boyfriend Bert.
but no one shows up – i keep waiting.
i watch and wait
chasing the ball in between.
guess today, i won't have a date.
so i go to chase ball eighteen.

2:00 am

it's 2:00 am
i pretend i need to pee
so mommy gets up to take me
i hop up
and steal her warm spot on the bed
i am cozy pup.

pet stores

the real reason i go to the pet store
is for the rodents
especially what's called a fancy rat.
i love to watch them
and i think i could break into the display case and get
them out.
my mommy says i can't have a pet.
but they're only $22.99.
and i want one so bad.
but mommy says i would probably destroy the house,
chasing the rat all over the room, until i caught it.
maybe i will get a job
so i can buy myself a fancy rat.

tennis ball

i don't care that you've already thrown the tennis ball
two hundred times tonight;
please just throw it once more.
[ball plops in mommy's lap]

Victoria Gehman

fifteen squirrels

i saw fifteen of them squirrels
on my morning walk
i stalked and stalked
almost had one twice
but they all got away
tomorrow, i say –
i will catch one tomorrow.
if only mom would set me free,
i'd climb that tree
and catch them squirrels.

exclusive

so much drama at the dog park –
Daisy broke up with Hank
because Hank cheated on her with Hattie
Hank also claims Ellie Mae is the love of his life –
how does he have three girls at once?
but me and Bert – we've been exclusive
since pretty much the day we met.

couch thieves

"quick," says one dog to the other,
"it looks like mother and father –
they're about to sit.
let's take their spots so they no longer fit."
hoomans must sit on the floor,
even if they get sore,
for the sofa is our domain
and we will reign;
they call us couch thieves,
but we prefer to be known as fur-niture queens.

dogs.

they love unconditionally.

they sit quietly with us when we are sad.

they stay when others walk away.

they are our best friends when others bully us.

they don't run from our tears; they just lick them away.

they give hugs when we feel lonely.

they give us purpose and a reason to live.

they give us a reason to go outside and get fresh air.

they leave muddy paw prints all over the house

and forever paw prints on our hearts.

they make us smile when we feel sad.

dogs make better friends than most humans.

and humans could learn a lot from them.

Other Books by Victoria:

Slow Your Pace, Hope a little Longer: a collection of poems
Available on Amazon and Barnes and Noble

Finding Hope in Changing Seasons
Available on Bookshop.org, Amazon, and at a local to
Lancaster, PA bookstore: Aaron's Books

Connect with Victoria:

www.writetoreconnect.com
Instagram: @writetoreconnect

If you enjoyed this book, I would love for you to leave
a review. Reviews truly do make a difference, and I so
appreciate your support.

Follow on Instagram to stay up to date on future books!